PERSPECTIVE
Made Easy

David R. Morin

J. Weston Walch, Publisher
Portland, Maine

DEDICATION

This set is dedicated to my parents whose love and encouragement enabled me to be what I wanted to be—an artist.

1   2   3   4   5   6   7   8   9   10

ISBN 0-8251-0018-6
Copyright © 1985
J. Weston Walch, Publisher
P.O. Box 658 • Portland, Maine 04104-0658

Printed in the United States of America

CONTENTS

INTRODUCTION

The subject of *perspective* often sounds rather frightening if you think of it as mechanical plans, projections, points, lines, theories, measurements, and mathematics (not to mention some almost unpronounceable terms). This set is not about the perspective used in technical drawing but is rather about the forms of perspective generally called freehand and linear. Sure, there will be lines, points, terms, and, I suppose, some form of math in the lessons, but frightening. . .? I didn't intend it to be that way.

Why study perspective? A lot of people and even some artists think that the mere ability to draw makes a person an artist. That's not totally accurate. A good artist has the ability to draw, of course, but he or she also possesses the knowledge of composition, design, color, and even perspective—in other words, all the "tools of the trade."

The rules of perspective are fairly simple to understand and to use. However, their worth and effectiveness are proportionate to the amount of time spent practicing them. The French romantic painter Delacroix (1798–1863) said that genius must always change the tenets of perspective. He meant that if a painter always followed the laws of perspective, then the resulting painting would probably not be a masterpiece. Perhaps he was correct. Many masterpieces are not correct perspectively. But to change perspective to meet your needs you must first know perspective. You can't change what you don't know.

This set will let you know about perspective. And here's a hint—DRAW, DRAW, DRAW! Keep a sketchbook with you whenever possible. Sketch interesting perspective problems, and complex forms, and sketch in different locations. Keep practicing.

Here's another hint about perspective: study other artists' works to see how they used perspective in their pictures or paintings. You could even check their perspective by putting a piece of tracing paper over a reproduction of their work and sketching in the PERSPECTIVE LINES, HORIZON LINES, VANISHING POINTS, and so on. That way you will be able to see how they constructed their pictures and whether or not they deviated from the rules of perspective—and, if so, just how much.

The general idea is to use this set as a basic guideline. Then keep practicing.

INTRODUCING PERSPECTIVE

PERSPECTIVE is the method we use to represent a three-dimensional object such as a table

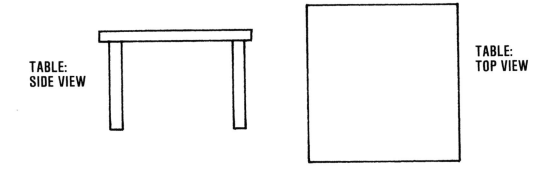

TABLE:
SIDE VIEW

TABLE:
TOP VIEW

on a two dimensional plane such as paper.

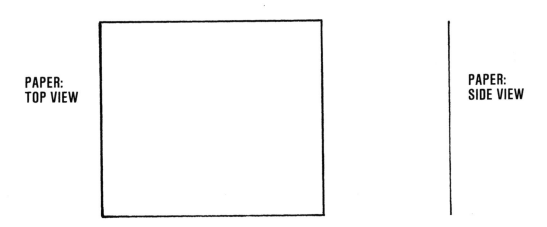

PAPER:
TOP VIEW

PAPER:
SIDE VIEW

THREE-DIMENSIONAL VIEW

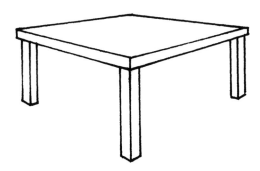

It is certainly possible and really quite easy to draw a solid, three-dimensional table on a sheet of paper and have the illusion of three-dimensionality: depth, direction, and distance. All you need to do is to follow the rules of PERSPECTIVE. With these rules and with practice you will be able to create an illusion to fool the eye.

The real secret to successful perspective drawing (and all other drawing and painting as well) is to OBSERVE. . .DRAW. . .PRACTICE. . .PRACTICE . . .and MORE OF THE SAME.

EQUIPMENT

Here are some pieces of equipment that you will need to do the perspective drawings.

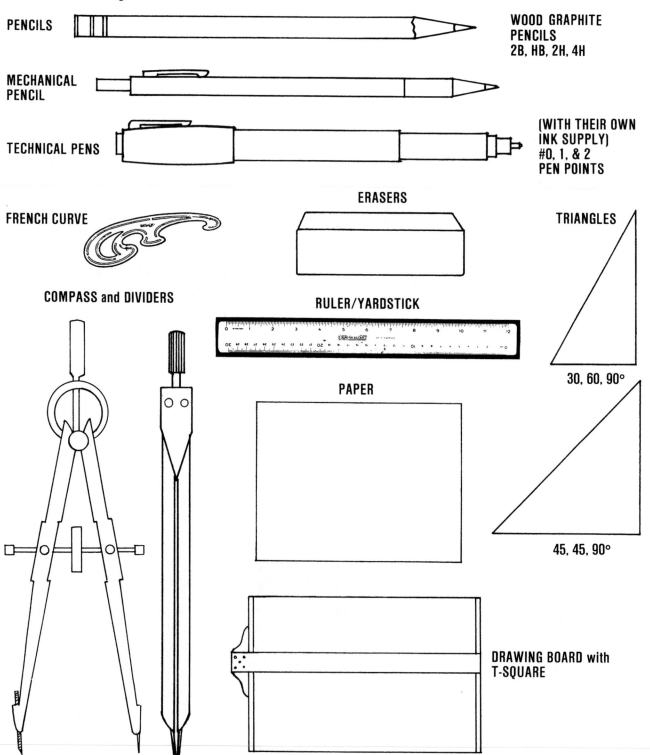

PENCILS

WOOD GRAPHITE PENCILS 2B, HB, 2H, 4H

MECHANICAL PENCIL

TECHNICAL PENS

(WITH THEIR OWN INK SUPPLY) #0, 1, & 2 PEN POINTS

ERASERS

FRENCH CURVE

TRIANGLES

COMPASS and DIVIDERS

RULER/YARDSTICK

30, 60, 90°

PAPER

45, 45, 90°

DRAWING BOARD with T-SQUARE

AERIAL PERSPECTIVE and COLOR PERSPECTIVE

AERIAL PERSPECTIVE concerns itself with air and the effects it has on objects in the distance. It is basically a fine arts perspective because it is so closely associated with color and landscapes.

Here are some general rules and observations about AERIAL PERSPECTIVE:

- Usually colors tend to become cooler and are less brilliant the farther away from the observer they are.
- An object's outline and detail are less defined, less clear as the object appears to recede.
- The differences in tone values of light and shade become less apparent in the far distance.
- The amount of moisture, smoke, and other atmospheric conditions, as well as distance, affect an object's color and definition.
- In black and white illustrations bold contrast is used in the foreground and various grays and blending of tones for the far distance.

NOTE: A word or two are necessary here about perspective in fine arts. Fine artists rarely try for mathematically correct perspective in every portion of their usually complex paintings. Yet you will find that their guidelines or underpaintings *are* drawn accurately. The theory is that the more accurate the guidelines, the easier it is to stay within certain boundaries or to deviate effectively from them. The distortions in perspective should definitely be deliberate and controlled rather than purely accidental. A mistake in perspective is certainly noticeable and makes a painting look very amateurish.

THINGS TO DO: Find an example from the work of a well-known artist who uses unnatural perspective methods—for example, one who exaggerates aerial perspective.

LINEAR PERSPECTIVE

This is the perspective system which we will be studying. LINEAR PERSPECTIVE refers to the apparent changes in the *size* of things caused by distance. Objects in the background or receding in the distance appear to diminish in size. The cubes below are all three feet high, wide, and deep. Yet as they recede toward the HORIZON the farthest one seems to become just a dot.

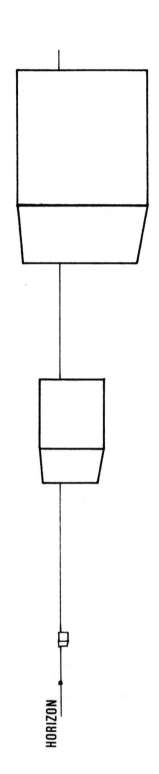

HORIZON

PICTURE PLANE

The PICTURE PLANE (referred to by the letters *PP*) can be thought of as an imaginary transparent plane (much like a piece of glass) located between the observer (called *S*) and the object being viewed. It is a vertical plane (up-and-down), and as the illustration shows, it can also correspond to the plane on which you could paint or draw the object you are viewing.

NOTE: Notice the lines from the observer to the object. What would happen to the size of the object on the PICTURE PLANE if the PLANE were moved farther away from the object?

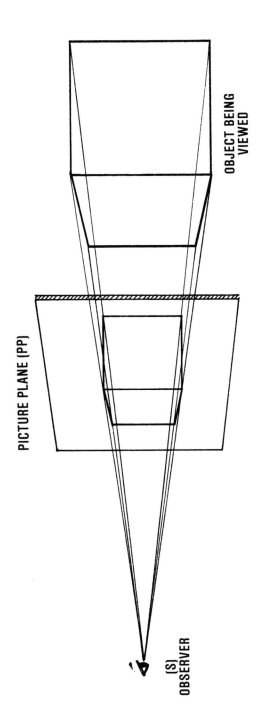

PICTURE PLANE (PP)

OBJECT BEING VIEWED

(S)
OBSERVER

HORIZON LINE

The HORIZON LINE is usually designated by the letters HL. HORIZON is the place where the curvature of the earth prevents us from seeing farther. In a picture the HORIZON LINE could be thought of as always being straight and always horizontal. The *position* it occupies in the picture is very changeable, as we will see. There are only a few things to remember about the HORIZON LINE:

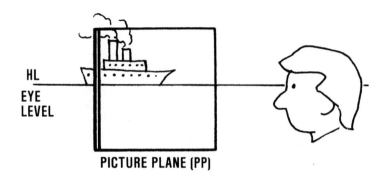

The HORIZON LINE is always at *your* eye level. It will be a bit different for someone who is over seven feet tall, but it will still be that person's HORIZON LINE at his or her eye level.

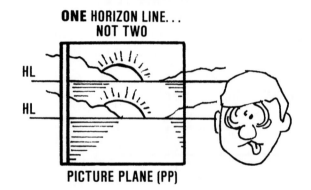

There is only one true HORIZON LINE in a picture.

The HORIZON LINE can certainly be above or below the limits of the PIC-TURE PLANE.

EYE LEVEL

EYE LEVEL is the height of the artist's eyes from the ground. You, the observer, can turn in any direction, and the horizon will always be at your eye level. Therefore, if the HORIZON LINE is high on the PICTURE PLANE, that usually means that the observer is high off the ground. If the HORIZON LINE is low, then the observer is probably low.

BIRD'S-EYE VIEW

NORMAL VIEW

WORM'S-EYE VIEW

SOME EYE LEVEL EXAMPLES

If a box is below EYE LEVEL/HORIZON LINE, then you will see the top.

a.

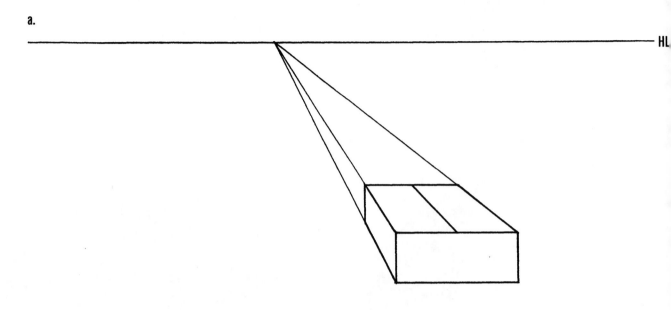

— HL

If a box is above EYE LEVEL, then you see the bottom.

b.

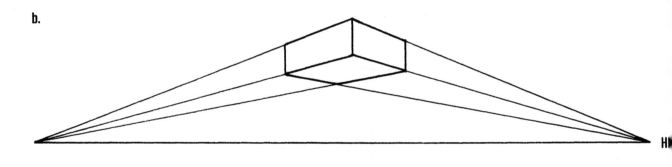

— H

If a box is exactly at EYE LEVEL, you see neither top nor bottom but only the side(s).

c.

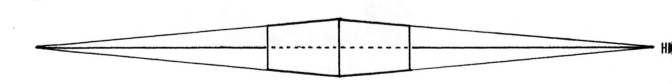

— H

POINT OF STATION, POINT OF SIGHT, and HORIZONTAL PLANE

When doing a perspective drawing, you should remember that it will be made from one specific spot called the POINT OF STATION (S), also called STATION POINT (SP). That spot corresponds to the eye of the observer.

The POINT OF SIGHT (P) is that point on the HORIZON LINE that is directly opposite the POINT OF STATION (S).

As shown in the illustration, the HORIZONTAL PLANE is the plane that is horizontal to the ground and is at eye level.

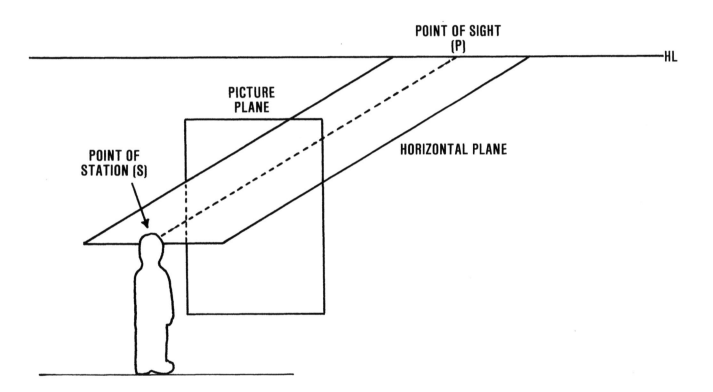

LINE OF VISION and GROUND LINE

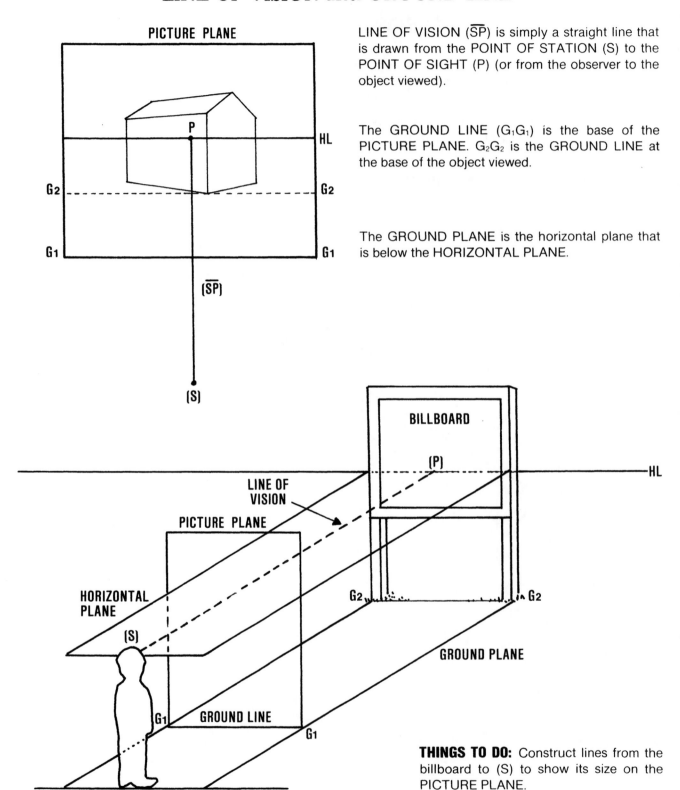

LINE OF VISION ($\overline{SP}$) is simply a straight line that is drawn from the POINT OF STATION (S) to the POINT OF SIGHT (P) (or from the observer to the object viewed).

The GROUND LINE (G_1G_1) is the base of the PICTURE PLANE. G_2G_2 is the GROUND LINE at the base of the object viewed.

The GROUND PLANE is the horizontal plane that is below the HORIZONTAL PLANE.

THINGS TO DO: Construct lines from the billboard to (S) to show its size on the PICTURE PLANE.

VANISHING POINT

As has been noted earlier, one of the principles of LINEAR PERSPECTIVE is that objects appear to become smaller as they recede into the distance. If an object goes far enough into the distance, it becomes just a dot and then finally just vanishes. This point is called the VANISHING POINT, or VP for short.

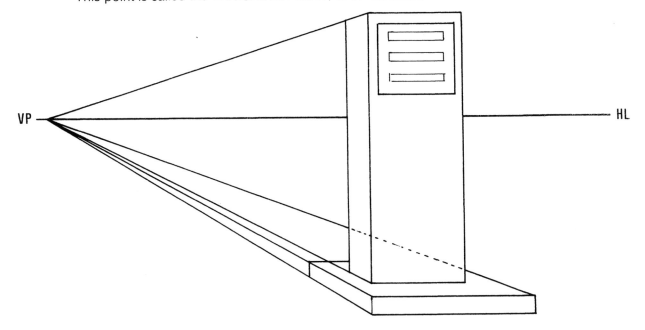

- The VANISHING POINT is the point where parallel lines appear to meet.
- The VP is always on the HORIZON LINE (HL).
- If two parallel lines meet at a VANISHING POINT, then all lines that are parallel to these lines will meet at the same VANISHING POINT.

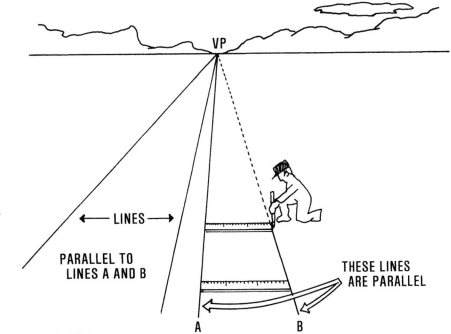

VANISHING POINT

A VANISHING POINT (like the HORIZON LINE) does *not* have to be within the PICTURE PLANE and frequently is not.

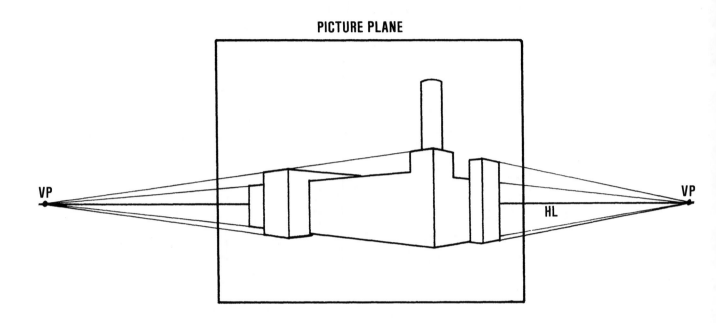

Unlike the HORIZON LINE, there may be many VANISHING POINTS in one picture or scene.

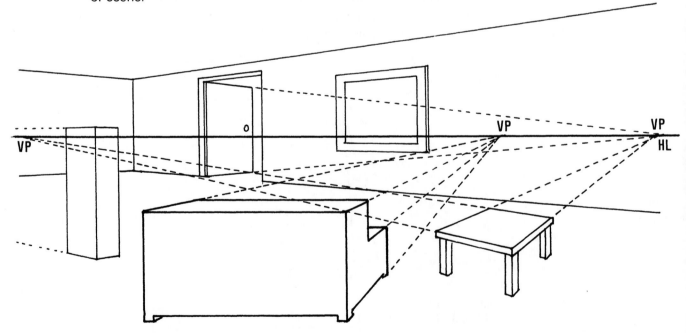

VANISHING POINT

Objects that are above the HORIZON LINE will generally have perspective lines that converge downward toward the VP. Objects that are below the HORIZON LINE will generally have lines that converge upwards.

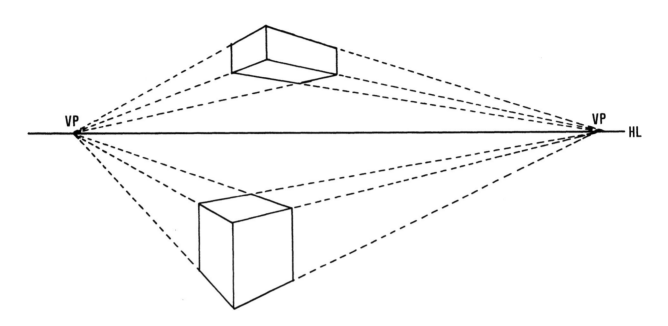

An important characteristic of perspective to remember is that when lines are drawn from the POINT OF STATION (S) to each VANISHING POINT of a rectangular or square figure, they always form a 90-degree angle.

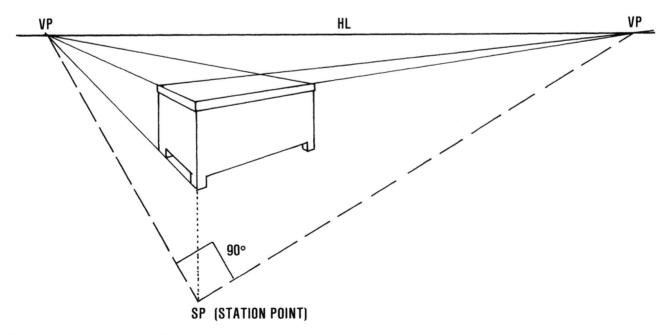

VANISHING POINT—
INACCESSIBLE

Sometimes a VANISHING POINT might be far beyond the limits of the paper you're using. You need to know where to put the VP so you can finish the drawing with some degree of accuracy.

Try a tack, a yardstick, and a little more paper. You could also work something out with a tack and some string.

VANISHING POINTS don't have to be inaccessible.

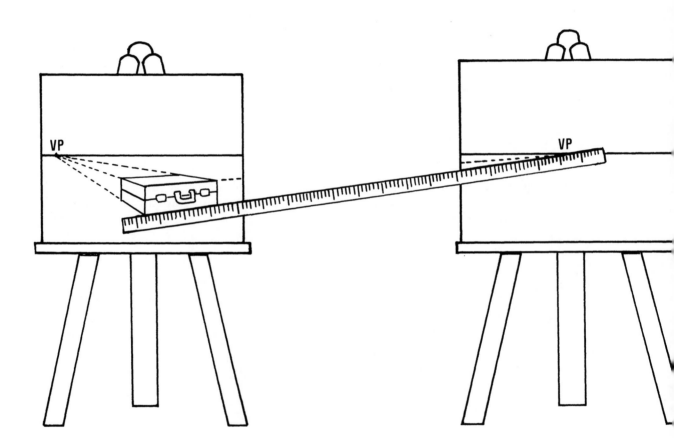

ONE-POINT PERSPECTIVE

ONE-POINT PERSPECTIVE occurs when the object that is viewed is *parallel* to the viewer. Another way to think of ONE-POINT PERSPECTIVE is *flat*, because whatever you are looking at has not been turned at an angle to you and the PICTURE PLANE.

The only problem encountered with ONE-POINT PERSPECTIVE is on deciding how far up or down the EYE LEVEL is in relation to the object. Just remember that the position of your eyes is also the location of the VANISHING POINT in ONE-POINT PERSPECTIVE.

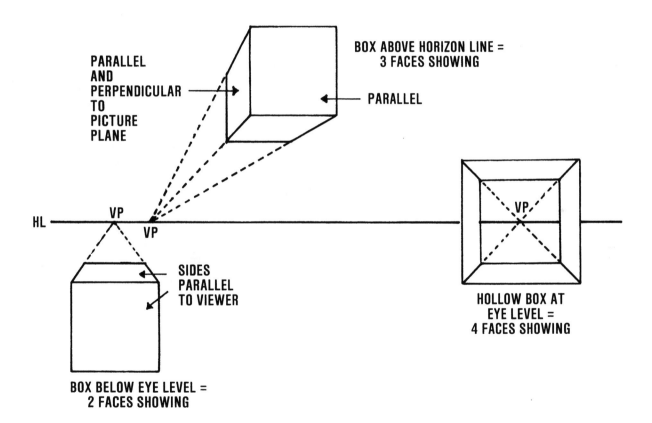

PARALLEL AND PERPENDICULAR TO PICTURE PLANE

BOX ABOVE HORIZON LINE = 3 FACES SHOWING

PARALLEL

HL   VP   VP

SIDES PARALLEL TO VIEWER

BOX BELOW EYE LEVEL = 2 FACES SHOWING

VP

HOLLOW BOX AT EYE LEVEL = 4 FACES SHOWING

ONE-POINT PERSPECTIVE
(continued)

Remember—only one VANISHING POINT on the HORIZON LINE.

One other part of ONE-POINT PERSPECTIVE that requires the artist's judgment (and practice) is deciding how far apart to place the parallel planes of the front surface or those lines that do *not* converge to a VANISHING POINT.

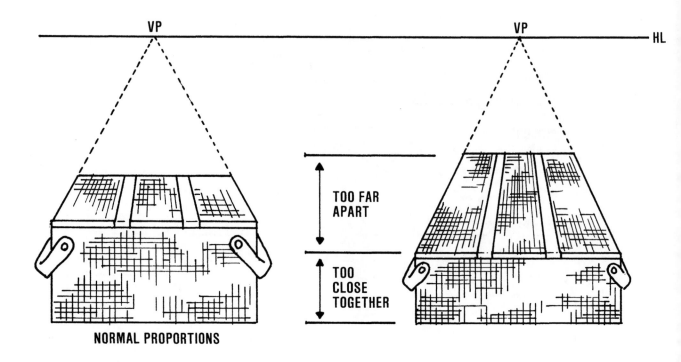

THINGS TO DO: Try a few one-point perspective drawings, varying the width of the parallel lines that do not converge.

ONE-POINT PERSPECTIVE—
Placing the HORIZON LINE and VANISHING POINT

NOTE: the guidelines about placement of the HORIZON LINE (HL) depend on the height of the viewing position.

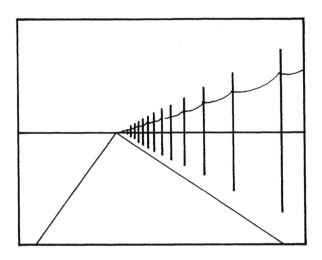

When the HORIZON LINE is nearly centered on the PICTURE PLANE, it means that the observer is about at the center as well.

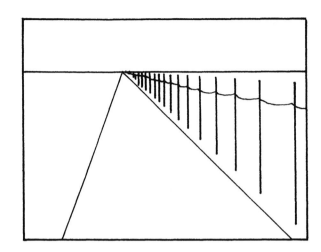

When the HORIZON LINE is high, it usually means that the observer is also viewing the scene at a higher vantage point than normal.

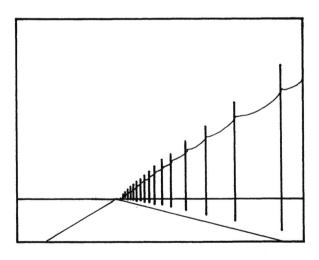

When the HORIZON LINE is low on the PICTURE PLANE, that usually means that the observer is also low to the ground.

VANISHING POINT SHOULD BE WITHIN THIS AREA

One method that you can use to avoid extreme distortion is to locate the central vanishing point in the middle third of the picture.

ONE-POINT PERSPECTIVE—
Some Scenes That Look Hard. . .But Aren't

BUILDINGS   **STREET SCENE**

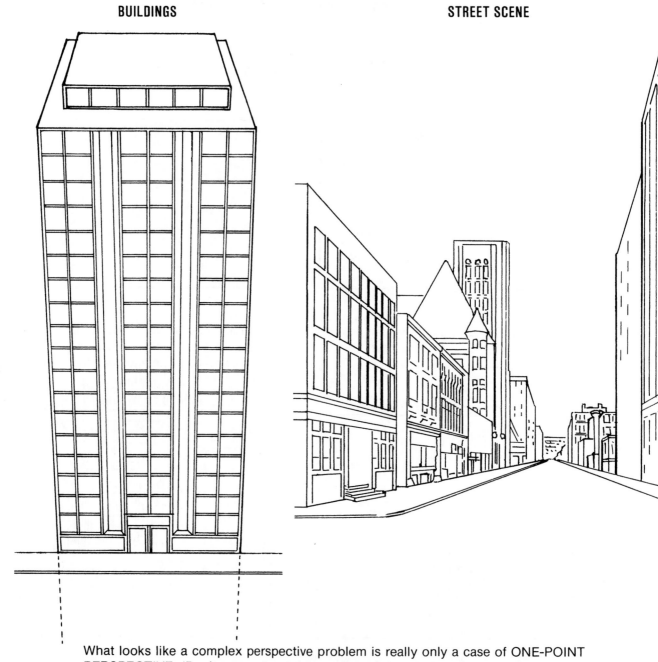

What looks like a complex perspective problem is really only a case of ONE-POINT PERSPECTIVE. (Don't worry about the spacing of the windows just yet. That's called PROPORTIONAL SPACING, and we will study that later.)

THINGS TO DO: Find some photographs of buildings. With a tissue overlay, find the VANISHING POINT of each.

TWO-POINT PERSPECTIVE

This is the most commonly used form of perspective.

TWO-POINT PERSPECTIVE is used for objects that are diagonal to the observer.

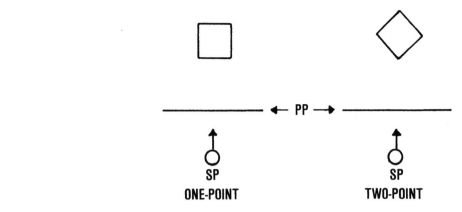

Objects in TWO-POINT PERSPECTIVE will have two VANISHING POINTS.

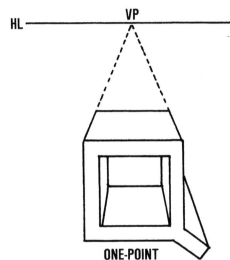

TWO-POINT PERSPECTIVE is more useful to the artist than ONE-POINT because most forms appear turned at various angles rather than lined up parallel.

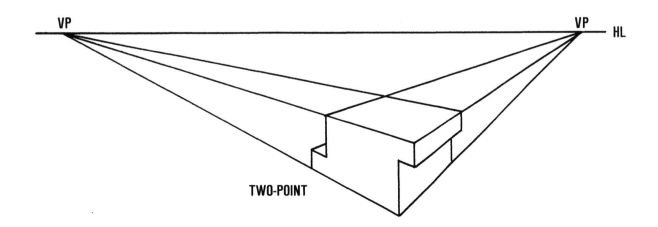

TWO-POINT PERSPECTIVE—
VANISHING POINTS

A significant problem with TWO-POINT PERSPECTIVE is how far apart to put the VANISHING POINTS.

There is a tendency to put the VANISHING POINTS too close to each other on the HORIZON LINE. If they are too close, then extreme FORESHORTENING results; the view becomes distorted and quite unnatural. This finished illustration looks OK. . .angles aren't too bad. . .table legs are the right dimensions. . .the perspective works.

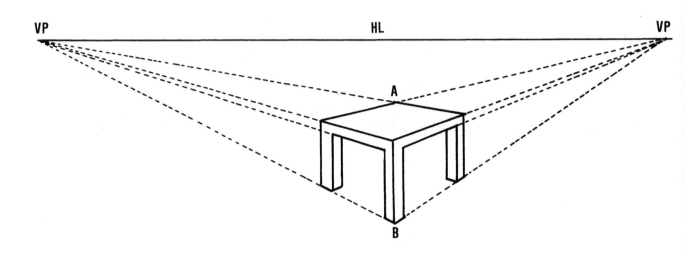

THINGS TO DO: You finish the table that has been started below. The left and right VANISHING POINTS are given for you as well as the front leg of the table. You finish drawing the rest of the table in perspective. How does it look? How could it look better?

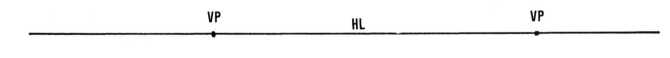

TWO-POINT PERSPECTIVE—
VANISHING POINT ON AN INCLINED PLANE

INCLINED PLANES (or *sloping lines*) can best be demonstrated with a drawing of the roof of a house.

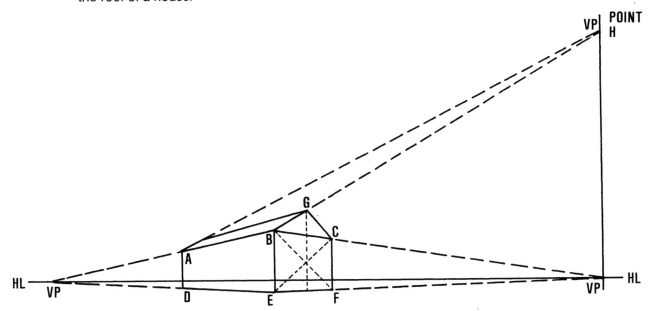

First draw the bottom of the house in perspective using the TWO-POINT PER-SPECTIVE previously covered. As a reminder, here are the steps used to create the bottom portion: draw the HORIZON LINE, establish the height of BE, locate the VP's, draw in the perspective lines from point E to the left VP and from E to the right VP, and also from point B to the left VP and right VP. From these lines you should be able to determine the width and the length of the house by drawing in the vertical AD and CF.

Next you will need to find the center of the front of the house, BCFE, and you can do that by drawing diagonal lines from corner to corner, lines BF and EC. The point where they intersect is the center you are looking for. Draw a vertical line through that center, and extend the line beyond the wall.

Again you make a visual estimate of how high the point of the roof should be and call that point G. Draw a perspective line from corner point B, through point G, and continue until beyond the area of the right VP. Draw a vertical line from the VP up until it intersects. Call this point H. Now you can connect point H to corner point A to determine the farther edge of the roof.

Point H is called an ACCIDENTAL VANISHING POINT because it does not lie on the HORIZON LINE as the two main VANISHING POINTS do. Yet it is still the focus point for the perspective lines of the roof.

THINGS TO DO: Draw a house in perspective. Add shingles to the roof and to the side of the house. Next try drawing a house with gambrel roof (one with two differ-ent inclined planes). Draw a book leaning against a table leg.

INCLINED PLANES—
ACCIDENTAL VANISHING POINTS

Probably the most basic of rules concerning INCLINED PLANES is that the ACCI-DENTAL VANISHING POINT lies directly above or below the VANISHING POINT on the HORIZON LINE.

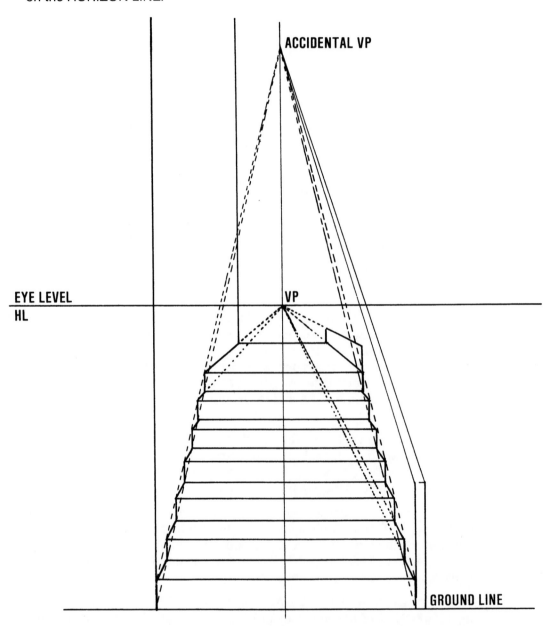

THINGS TO DO: The stairway shown above is in ONE-POINT PERSPECTIVE. Add the stairway that turns right at the landing; continue upward until you run out of paper (at least another half dozen stairs). Stairways are not difficult to draw. Notice the relationship of both the PERSPECTIVE LINES and the VP's. Add a few banisters to the railing. Continue the railing to match the stairs you draw.

THE FALSE HORIZON LINE and VANISHING POINT

Just when you thought you knew all about HORIZON LINES and VANISHING POINTS, you find out that some are false! In the illustration below, the buildings have the same VANISHING POINT on the HORIZON LINE, the "true" HL. The street and the sidewalks converge to a FALSE VANISHING POINT. Can you see why?

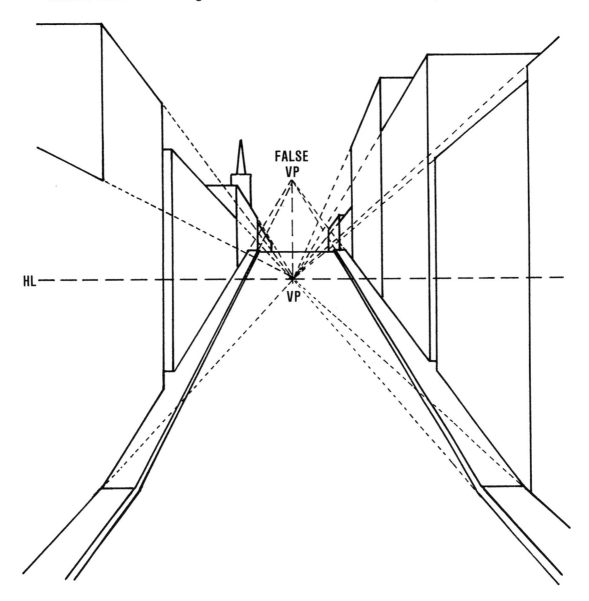

THINGS TO DO: Try your own street scene, but keep it simple at first. Try one that shows a dip in the street rather than a hill. Don't worry about drawing in windows right now.

THINGS TO DO IN THE FUTURE: After you've completed the lesson on EQUAL-DISTANCE PERSPECTIVE you should come back to this lesson and draw in the doorways and the windows for the buildings.

TWO-POINT PERSPECTIVE—
THE MOVING OBSERVER

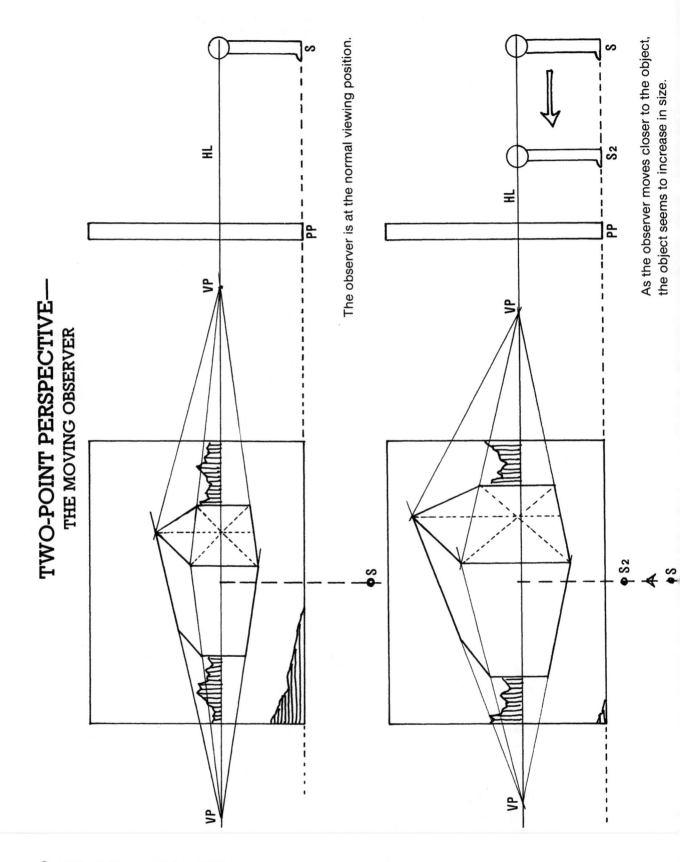

The observer is at the normal viewing position.

As the observer moves closer to the object, the object seems to increase in size.

TWO-POINT PERSPECTIVE—
THE MOVING OBSERVER (continued)

As the observer goes higher, the HORIZON LINE is raised.

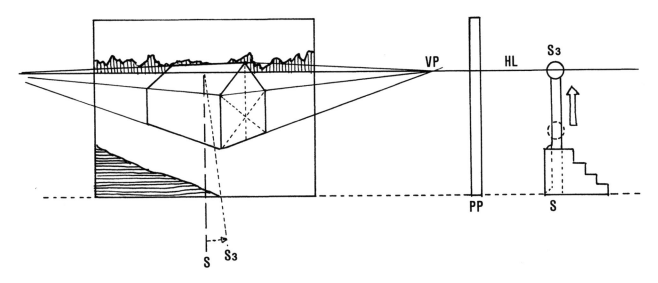

In this illustration the observer has moved to the left.

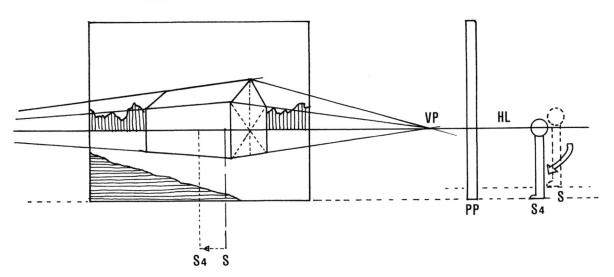

THINGS TO DO: Show what would happen if the observer at the "normal" viewing height moves either to the left or to the right and *back* all at the same time. Try a couple of other different movement combinations, including lower.

THREE-POINT PERSPECTIVE

When an object or scene is viewed and none of the edges are parallel to the PIC-TURE PLANE, then the result is THREE-POINT PERSPECTIVE. In THREE-POINT PERSPECTIVE there are also three VANISHING POINTS.

THREE-POINT is the least used of all perspectives. It is most often used to empha-size a feeling of height in a picture.

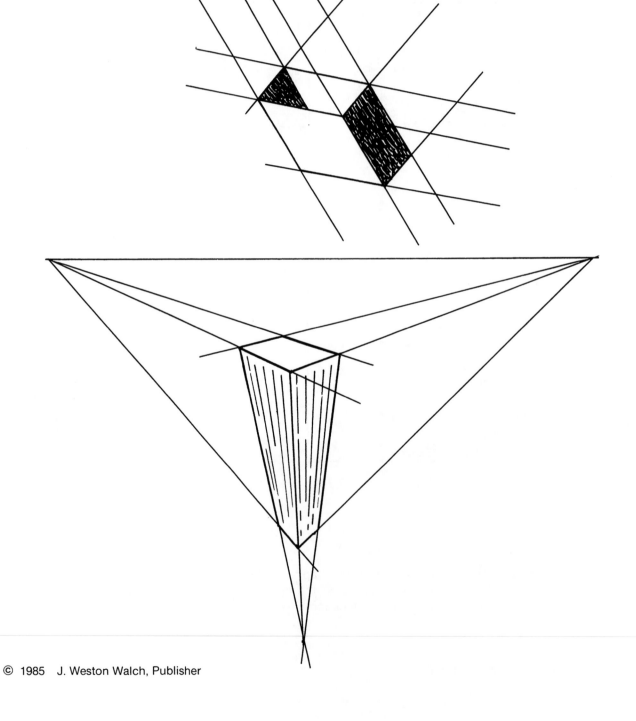

ACCURATE MEASUREMENT WITHOUT OBSERVATION

Your assignment is to draw the "perfect" CUBE. So far we have learned to draw CUBES in perspective, but have they been CUBES? Maybe they were more rectangular, or less than square, perspectively speaking. This lesson on ACCURATE MEASUREMENT will add to your knowledge of perspective. This is a CUBE in TWO-POINT PERSPECTIVE.

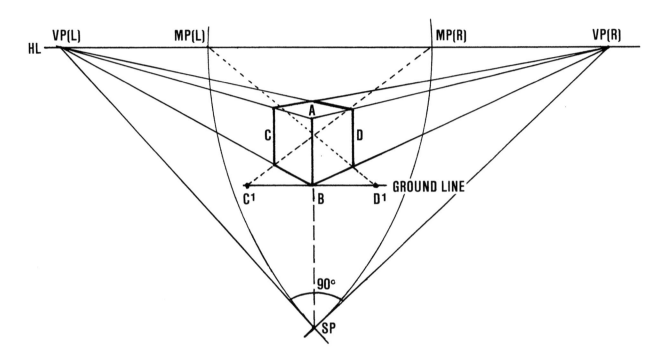

1. Draw the HL and the two VANISHING POINTS.

2. Determine the height of the CUBE you are going to draw, and call it AB. You should consider this line to be in the PICTURE PLANE or at least parallel to it.

3. We should have a STATION POINT somewhere, so draw a vertical line down from point B. Because the STATION POINT always forms a 90° angle to the VP's, locating the STATION POINT shouldn't be too difficult if we use a triangle with a 90° angle.

4. From points A and B draw lines to each of the VANISHING POINTS. *NOTE:* At this point the problem is to determine where lines C and D will be located. If we put them in the wrong place, the drawing will be a rectangle and not a CUBE. Read on.

5. To establish C and D, we must draw a horizontal GROUND LINE. Notice that this line is parallel to the PICTURE PLANE. That means that any measurements on this line should be accurate if we are careful about measuring.

6. Measure on the GROUND LINE distances BC¹ and BD¹ that are equal to the height of the cube, AB.

7. Now we establish MEASURING POINTS by using a compass and swinging an ARC from the SP to the HL using the VP as the center. The intersection of the ARC and the HL locates MP(L) and MP(R).

8. From MP(L) draw a line to D¹. From MP(R) draw a line to C¹. The points at which these lines cross the base perspective lines locate the proper and accurate depth of the CUBE. Add some lines and the CUBE is finished.

ACCURATE PROPORTIONS
WITHOUT OBSERVATION

If you learned to do accurate measurement in the previous lesson, then the next logical step is to draw an object with the desired proportions, and to do it accurately in perspective. To draw a box that is 2' x 4' x 6' you will use pretty much the same steps as you did in the lesson before this.

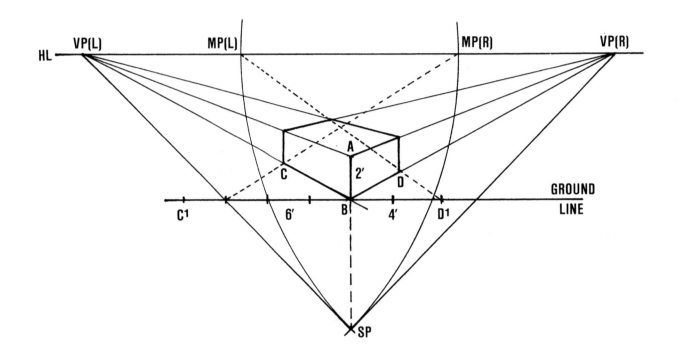

1. Draw the HORIZON LINE, the STATION POINT, and the VANISHING POINTS.
2. Draw AB. It now represents a measurement of 2'.
3. From A and B draw lines to the VP's, VP(L) and VP(R).
4. Draw the ground line.
5. Using AB as a guide, mark off 4' and 6' on the GROUND LINE.
6. Using the VP as a center, swing ARCS to the HORIZON LINE from the STATION POINT. These establish the measuring points, MP(L) and MP(R).
7. From MP(L) draw a line to D¹. The intersection of this line with the B–VP(R) line will be point D. This length is the correct and accurate foreshortened projection of the 6' side BD¹.

THINGS TO DO: Keep practicing until you have the steps down and the theory well in hand. Then try expanding the box-shaped drawing into a house. Even add on a smaller garage next to it.

SUMMARY EXERCISE:
ONE- and TWO-POINT PERSPECTIVE

Redraw the boxes below and supply the missing perspective boxes where the arrows are. You should be able to draw at least half a dozen intermediate box sketches for each arrow. If you keep your boxes all on one page, going left to right as well as up and down, you will end up with a good-looking, well-designed page.

Each box should look as if the viewer had taken a step or two around it and had stopped to sketch it. The downward drawings should resemble a box that is falling off a table in very slow motion.

THINGS TO DO: Try drawing the boxes freehand as mentioned above. Then use your straightedge and triangle to check the perspective.

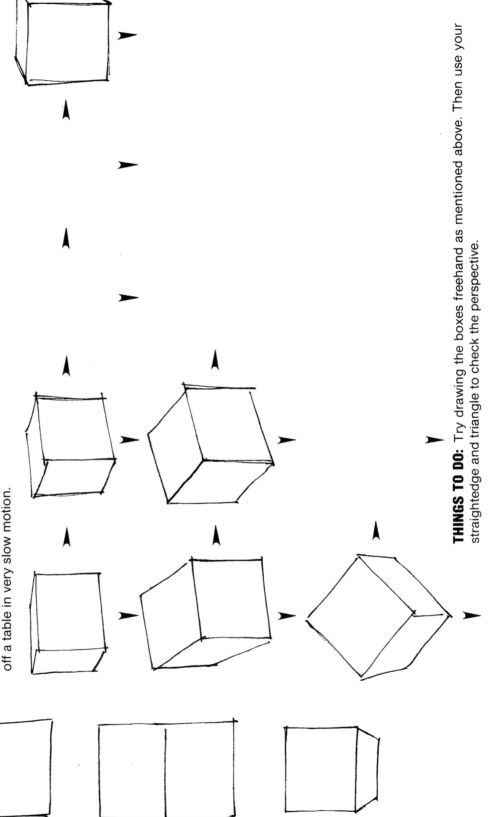

EQUAL DISTANCE PERSPECTIVE—
PROPORTIONAL SPACING

Did you ever wonder how you draw posts in perspective and spaced so that they look as if they actually fade into the distance? Well, here's a fairly easy way to accomplish the task.

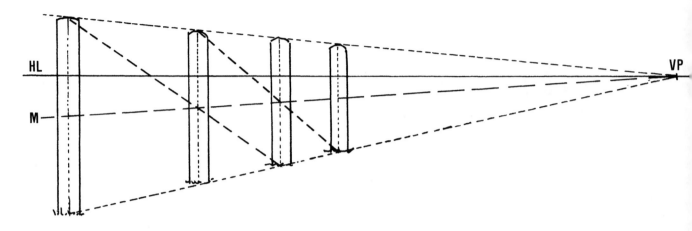

1. Draw a HORIZON LINE.
2. Draw a post. Draw a line along the top and bottom of that post to the VANISHING POINT on the horizon.
3. From the VP draw a line through the middle or center of the post.
4. Now it's time to draw in the second post. The distance this second post is from the first is totally up to you. You decide on the spacing.
5. After you've determined the location of the second post, you should draw a line from the top of the first post through the center of the second post all the way to the base line. Where that intersection occurs is where the third post will go.
6. Repeat the procedure for the third post, fourth, and so on.

THINGS TO DO: Finish the post illustration shown here. Then show some railroad tracks that fade into the distance. The procedure is the same, only this time you are drawing horizontal spacing.

PERSPECTIVE SPACING

Do you need to draw seven books in a row and in correct perspective? Here's how.

HL

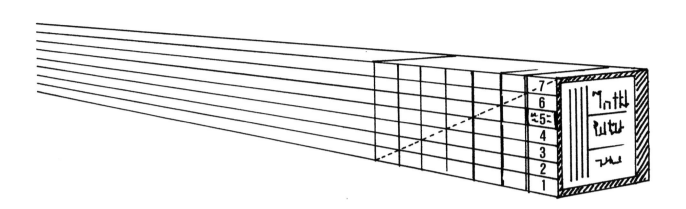

1. Block out a box in perspective and measure off seven equal spaces on the forward corner. Next draw the perspective lines to the HL (*not* shown in the illustration due to space limitations).

2. Connect the corners of the box with a diagonal line. Notice where the diagonal crosses. Draw in vertical lines, and you have an area that has been divided into seven perspectively correct spaces.

THINGS TO DO: What other things can be drawn using this new technique? How about the columns in front of a Greek temple? How about a checkerboard? Try one.

HOW TO FIND THE PERSPECTIVE CENTER

To find the PERSPECTIVE CENTER of a square, draw diagonals from one corner to the opposite corner. Where these lines meet is the center, horizontally and vertically. You can use this same principle for cubes and rectangles.

THE CENTER IN PERSPECTIVE

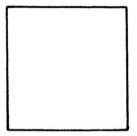 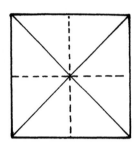 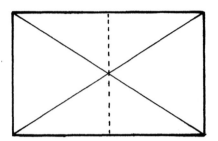

Drawing diagonals is also a method to divide a CUBE or a box into halves. What would happen if you divided the half in half? In half again? Try it on one of the faces of the drawing below.

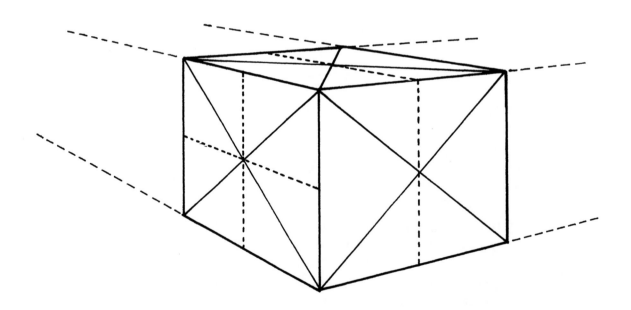

THINGS TO DO: Having divided a CUBE in half, make something out of it, like a cabinet with doors, or dice, or . . . .

THE MOVING VANISHING POINT

Here is an example of a VANISHING POINT that moves.

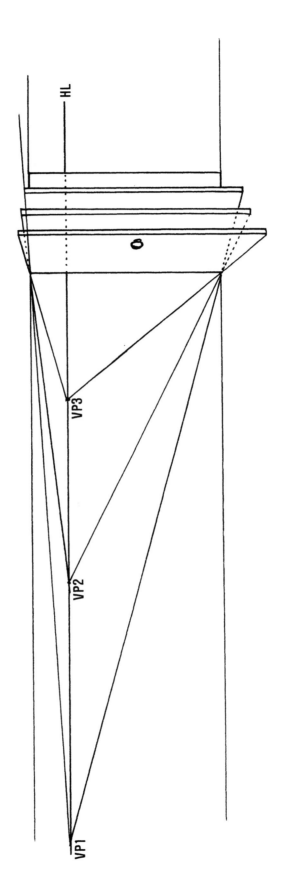

THINGS TO DO: You draw a moving vanishing point for another kind of door—*any* kind of door—and have it open from the side opposite the one in the illustration above. Can you think of any other objects or scenes that use MOVING VANISHING POINTS? Turning the illustration on its side may give you a hint (steps or stairs, hills, inclines, revolving doors, etc.).

THE PERSPECTIVE OF REFLECTIONS

A reflection can be thought of as an extension of the object in most cases. A reflection, therefore, will have the same VANISHING POINTS as the object. Illustrated is a CUBE in front of a mirror. The reflection appears as far beyond the mirror as the object is before it. As long as the object (in this case the CUBE of sugar) is seen in ONE-POINT PERSPECTIVE and the mirror is exactly parallel to the picture plane, then the reflection is quite easy to draw, as you can see.

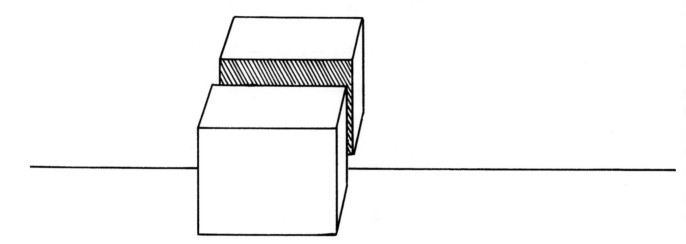

If the mirror is tilted or the object is turned to an awkward angle, then the reflection becomes much more difficult to draw.

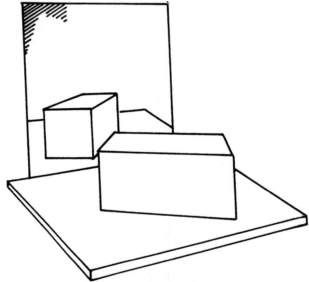

THINGS TO DO: Arrange a couple of books in front of a mirror. Look at the reflection, change your VP and SP by moving to a different location, and then sketch some freehand perspective scenes. Then try drawing the PERSPECTIVE LINES that you've learned about so far on the sketch or on a piece of tracing paper laid over the sketch. Try a couple of different views. How well do they match each other?

THE PERSPECTIVE OF REFLECTIONS

Here we see a building right on the bank of a lake. After drawing the building to correct perspective and determining the VANISHING POINT of the sloping roof, you will note that you can quickly determine the reflected VANISHING POINT because it is directly beneath the VANISHING POINT of the roof and at an equal distance below the HORIZON LINE.

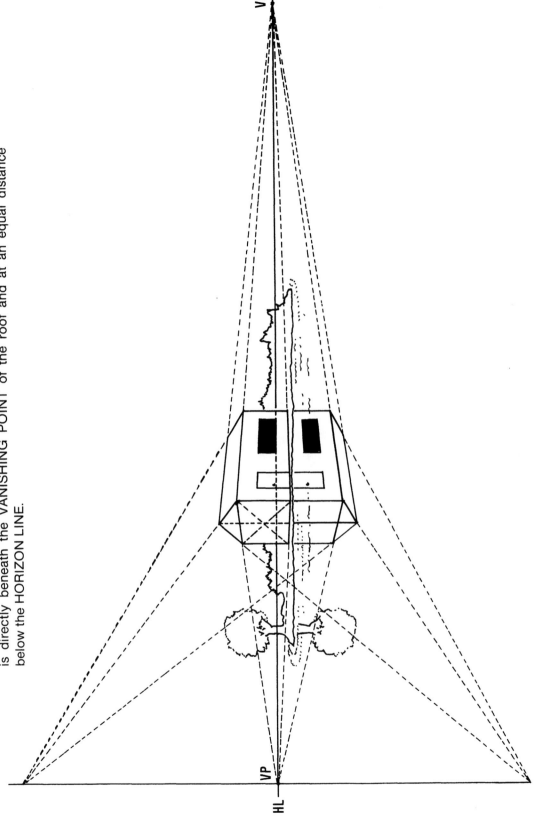

SHADOWS IN PERSPECTIVE (SUN)

Our natural light comes from the sun. Since the sun is such a great distance from us, we should consider its light rays as being *parallel*. This means that we can use the rules of perspective stating that PARALLEL LINES will meet at some common VANISHING POINT.

1. First, establish the HORIZON LINE (figure a).

2. Draw a simple vertical object, such as a billboard, and assume that the sun is in front of you and to your left.

3. Draw a vertical line from the sun's position (A) to the HORIZON LINE (B).

4. From this point you can draw the PERSPECTIVE (PARALLEL) LINES from point (B) on the GROUND PLANE to the billboard and beyond.

5. Next, draw lines from the sun (A) to the corners of the billboard until they intersect the lines of the GROUND PLANE at points C, D, E, and F.

6. Shade in the area and you will have a perfect shadow.

FIGURE a

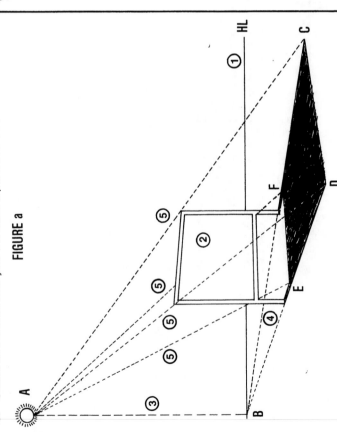

If you want to draw a shadow that indicates that the sun is *behind you*, you have to add some extra construction lines.

1. Establish the HORIZON LINE.

2. Draw a simple vertical object, such as a billboard.

3. Establish the position of the sun (A).

4. Draw a line from (A) diagonally through the billboard's corners, extending the line for some distance beyond the corner.

5. Draw a vertical line from the sun (A) to the HORIZON LINE and label that point (B). Now, using a ruler or a pair of dividers, measure the length of line AB.

6. Using this measurement draw a vertical line from the HORIZON to the diagonal line you drew for Step 3. Label the point on the HORIZON as (C) and the point on the diagonal as (D).

7. On the GROUND PLANE draw perspective lines from the legs of the billboard (X and Y) to (C) on the HORIZON LINE.

8. Next draw lines from (D) to the corners of the billboard (E, F, G, and H). These lines establish the intersection points for the billboard's shadow.

9. Shade in the area.

THINGS TO DO: Try moving the sun to a different location, either higher or lower, left or right. Try one with the sun directly over the billboard.

FIGURE b

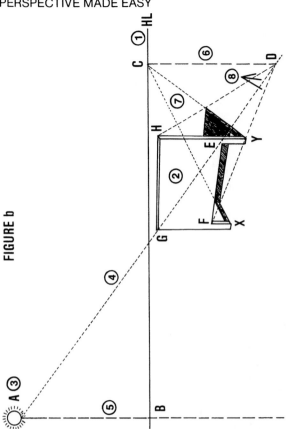

SHADOWS CAST BY A SOLID OBJECT IN SUNLIGHT

The basic theory shown in the previous lesson can be used again. The VANISHING
POINT for a shadow will be on the HORIZON LINE directly under the sun (VP). The
length of the shadow can now be determined by drawing perspective lines from the
sun to points on the object and extending them to the ground.

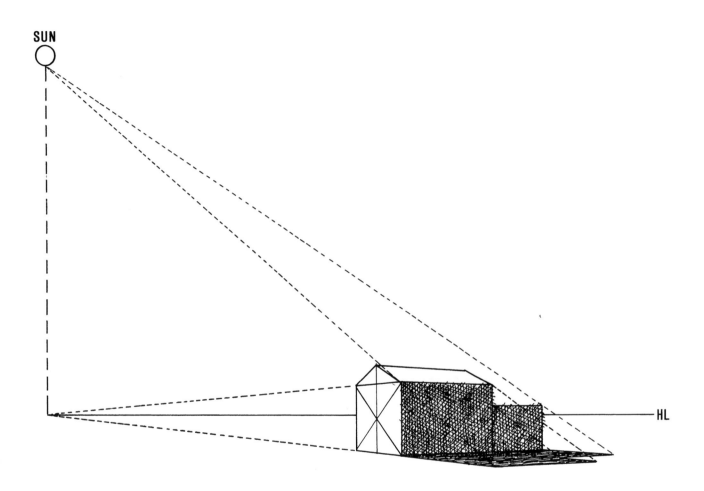

THINGS TO DO: As in the previous lesson on SHADOWS, practice moving the sun to
different locations. Try adding a chimney, a flag pole, or some other structure that
will create additional shadows.

SHADOWS IN PERSPECTIVE IN ARTIFICIAL LIGHT

The big difference between the sun and an artificial light source is that the light rays from artificial light are *not* parallel but radiate outward in all directions at once. The street light and other solid objects illustrate how these shadows have a VANISHING POINT that is directly beneath the light and not on the HORIZON LINE as with the sun.

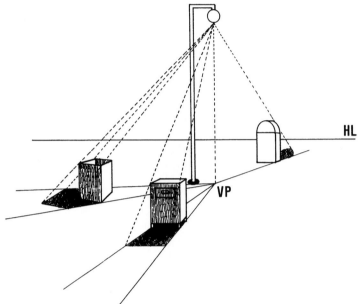

A light hanging from the ceiling presents a similar problem and solution. The VANISHING POINT for the light is similar to that for the street light in the illustration above, directly beneath the light source. Extending lines from the light outward to each object and continuing to the ground line (or a wall) provides the shadow proportions.

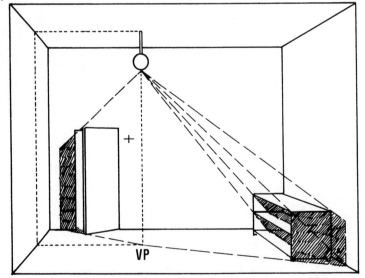

THINGS TO DO: Draw your own street light or room scene; put in a few differently shaped objects (figures, beachball, sofa, a tank, a banana, a parrot, etc.).

FIGURES IN PERSPECTIVE

Here is an easy way to construct figures at various positions in a picture. All of the figures are assumed to have the same height.

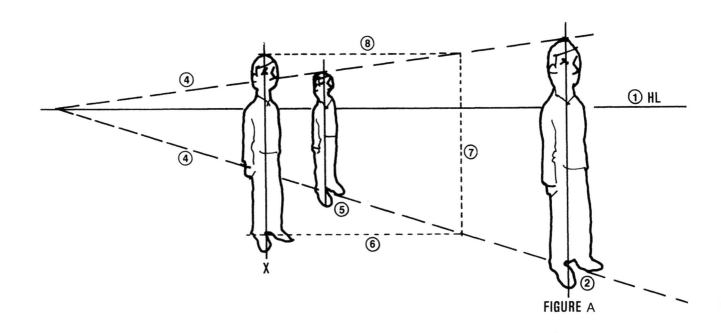

FIGURE A

1. Draw the HORIZON LINE.

2. Draw figure A. (Note that in this illustration the EYE LEVEL is at the figure's shoulder. That means that the person you are drawing is taller than you are.)

3. Establish a VANISHING POINT on the HORIZON LINE.

4. Draw the perspective lines from the figure to the VP.

5. You can now draw any figure using these two lines. Note that no matter where the figure is placed, the HORIZON LINE will always be at the person's shoulder level.

6. To draw a figure *not* on these PERSPECTIVE LINES, say at point X, draw a line parallel to the HORIZON LINE from point X until it meets the ground PERSPECTIVE LINE.

7. Draw a vertical line from this point until it reaches the top PERSPECTIVE LINE.

8. Draw another horizontal line parallel to the one drawn in step 6; start at the point where the vertical line drawn in step 7 meets the upper PERSPECTIVE LINE. You have now established the correct height for this slightly stand-offish person.

9. Finish the drawing of the figure.

THINGS TO DO: Using the illustration as a guide, add some additional figures to the drawing. You may want to add another VP to the right. Also it will be easier if you keep all the figures of similar height.

FIGURES TO SCALE WITH OTHER OBJECTS

You can determine other heights and perspectives by using a figure.

1. Draw a six-foot figure.
2. Establish the HL (at shoulder level again) and a distant VP.
3. Draw a perpendicular line upward through the figure, determining other six-foot units. (The illustration shows eighteen feet.)
4. You can now draw in other objects, such as the three-foot-high patio chair and an eighteen-foot-high building to scale and in perspective.

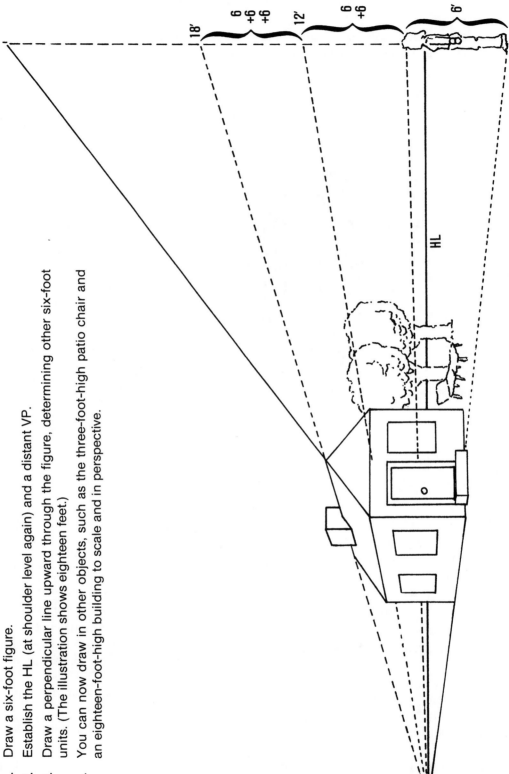

THINGS TO DO: Using this illustration or one of your own, put in some other objects, such as a four-foot child in back of the house, a five-foot person approaching the first figure, etc. Be imaginative!

FIGURES IN PERSPECTIVE: FORESHORTENING

FORESHORTENING is a special kind of problem in LINEAR PERSPECTIVE. It requires the drawing of a non-geometric, irregularly shaped object, namely the human form.

Unfortunately there is no set of rules governing foreshortening. It is a matter of observation, experience, and practice. What you do need is a thorough knowledge of human anatomy. Unless you know about form, it will be very difficult to fool the eye, and your drawing will look very distorted.

You will find that the foreshortened figure will probably need some sort of background as well. Here your accumulated knowledge of perspective will be helpful.

FORESHORTENING occurs when you draw (or paint) so as to make the lines of an object shorter than they actually are in order to give the illusion of proper relative size. Another way to think of FORESHORTENING is the change in shape that occurs when a form is turned away from the viewer. A good example is the view an ant has of you just before your shoe descends.

THINGS TO DO: People (figures) usually have a place in most drawings or paintings. Draw them whenever you have the chance, either from life or from photographs. Be especially aware of those poses that demonstrate foreshortening. Draw them, practice them, check them for accuracy.

CIRCLES IN PERSPECTIVE—
THE ELLIPSE

Up to now we have studied shapes with right angles. But the world around us also consists of CIRCLES or ARCS, and you should know how to draw them accurately. Drawing a perfect CIRCLE or even an ELLIPSE freehand is quite difficult, but with practice yours should look better and better. Your assignment right now is to draw an ELLIPSE, which is another term for a CIRCLE IN PERSPECTIVE.

The easiest way to draw a CIRCLE IN PERSPECTIVE is to put that ELLIPSE within a perspective square.

1. Establish the HORIZON LINE (HL).
2. Draw the square in perspective.
3. Draw the diagonals to determine the center.
4. Draw the horizontal and vertical center lines of the square AB and CD.
5. Sketch in the arcs of the CIRCLE so that they meet the four points of the center lines, A, B, C, and D.

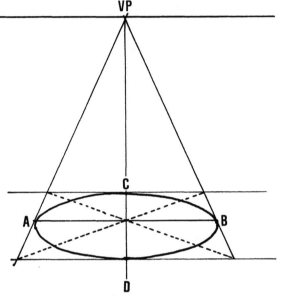

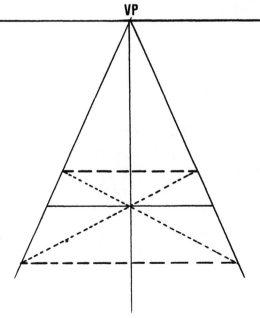

Using the illustration at the left, you draw in the ELLIPSE. Don't feel bad if it doesn't look too great the first few times; it's not as easy as it looks. If you can do it right off—terrific!

THINGS TO DO: Draw a couple of different perspective squares and then put in the CIRCLE. Try some squares that are *above* the HL.

DRAWING CIRCLES IN PERSPECTIVE

If you're having problems making your ELLIPSES look good, try this method.

The ARCH should meet the *diagonals* approximately one-third of the way in from the corners of the box. With enough practice you will probably not need to mark off the diagonals like this, but it is a valid method of obtaining the correct perspective.

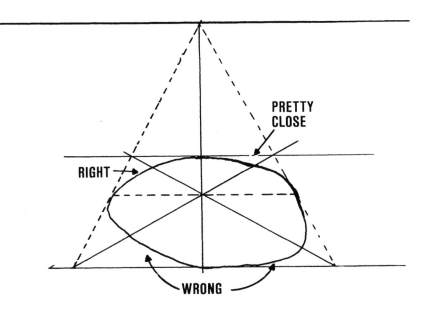

THINGS TO DO: When you need to draw a CIRCLE IN PERSPECTIVE, first draw the square. As you can see from the cube, it is relatively easy to finish drawing in the missing CIRCLES, so go ahead and do it. Next draw a box in TWO-POINT PERSPECTIVE and again inscribe CIRCLES on the box faces.

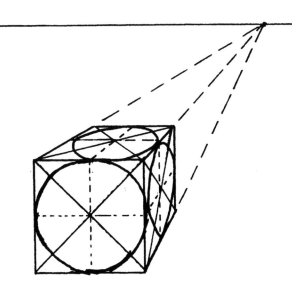

CYLINDERS

To draw a CYLINDER in perspective, first draw the rectangular box that encloses it. Note that the perspective CIRCLES you draw must and will have a common AXIS.

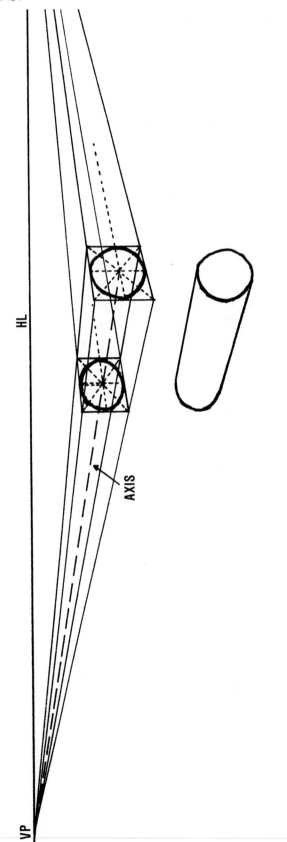

HL

VP

AXIS

THINGS TO DO: Using the illustration as a guide, try shortening or lengthening the AXIS to make the CYLINDER longer or shorter. Try using the CYLINDER as a guide for the wheels of an automobile. Imagine it is a tin can on its side and you have to draw a paper label on it in perspective.

HORIZONTAL CIRCLES

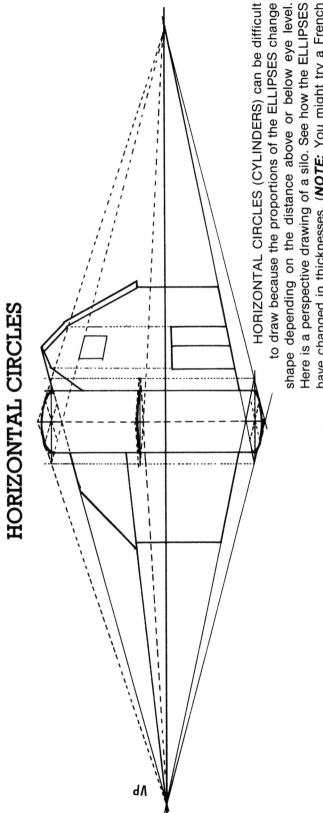

VP

HORIZONTAL CIRCLES (CYLINDERS) can be difficult to draw because the proportions of the ELLIPSES change shape depending on the distance above or below eye level. Here is a perspective drawing of a silo. See how the ELLIPSES have changed in thicknesses. (*NOTE:* You might try a French curve for smoother-looking ELLIPSES).

Here is how you can easily construct a coffee mug using the perspective principles you've learned so far. Something else you've learned is to do shadows. Shade the coffee mug, pretending that the sun is shining and is causing a long shadow on the ground.

THINGS TO DO: Try drawing the coffee mug at different eye levels. Then draw a cylindrical coffee pitcher with the lid partially open. Just keep in mind the INCLINED PLANE principle. Now try shading and shadowing these drawings.

DIVIDING A CIRCLE IN PERSPECTIVE

You've been asked to draw a clock face in perspective—and, of course, accurately. How do you do it?

Figure a.

1. Draw the square in perspective.
2. Draw the CIRCLE in perspective.
3. Extend horizontal lines A, B, and C from top, middle, and bottom of the circle.

Figure b.

4. At some point away from the CIRCLE draw a vertical line, DE.
5. Draw with a compass or a circle template the arc DFE.
6. Because you want to draw a clock face, divide the arc into six equal spaces. (**HINT:** use a 30°–60°–90° triangle to mark off the divisions.)
7. Next draw horizontal lines from these points to the vertical line on the clock face.

Figure c.

8. From the VP (not shown here) draw PERSPECTIVE LINES through the points on the vertical to the other side of the clock face. The lines intersecting the circle are where you will put the 12 clock numbers.
9. In less than ten steps you have a perfect clock face in perspective!

THINGS TO DO: Now that you've learned to divide a CIRCLE IN PERSPECTIVE, how many other objects can you draw? Try a gear with a dozen cogs. . .or a wagon wheel with spokes.

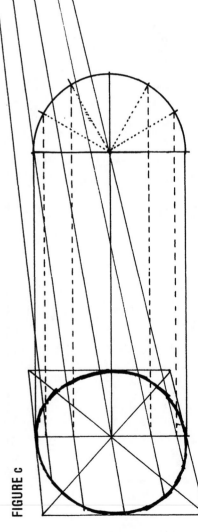

FIGURE a

FIGURE b

FIGURE c

CIRCLES IN PERSPECTIVE—ARCHES

An ARCH as used in this lesson is a semicircle. The same principles apply to this kind of perspective drawing as those previously learned. Here is a step-by-step diagram:

1. Draw the HORIZON LINE.

2. Draw a vertical that will represent the corner of the column.

3. Establish VANISHING POINTS, left and right. Keep at least *one* VP at a reasonable distance from the vertical, otherwise the drawing will look awkward.

4. Now draw perspective lines to the VANISHING POINTS.

5. Using the corner vertical as a guide establish the thickness of the column.

6. Now is a good time to determine the height of the archway.

7. You can also establish an arbitrary width of the archway.

8. Using the technique of inscribing a PERSPECTIVE CIRCLE inside a perspective square, draw the first rounded ARCH.

9. Utilizing EQUAL DISTANCE PERSPECTIVE, you can now determine placement of the next and successive columns.

THINGS TO DO: Finish another ARCH or two on the illustration or draw one with a different HL, VP, etc., yourself. Notice the space above the ARCHES in the illustration? Add something to this space using EQUAL-DISTANCE PERSPECTIVE—or better yet, more ARCHES.

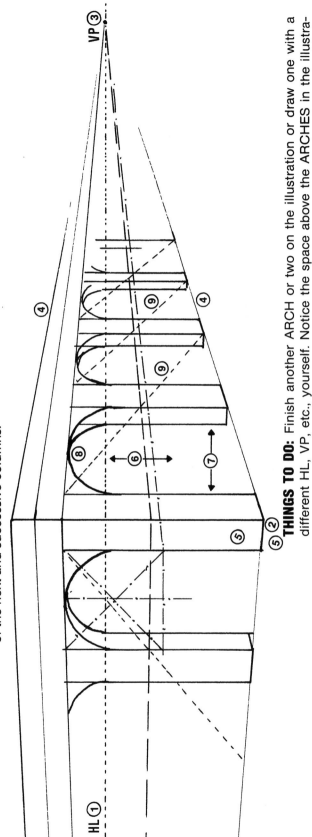

"ACTION" WITH PERSPECTIVE

Here we combine several perspective theories including FORESHORTENING.

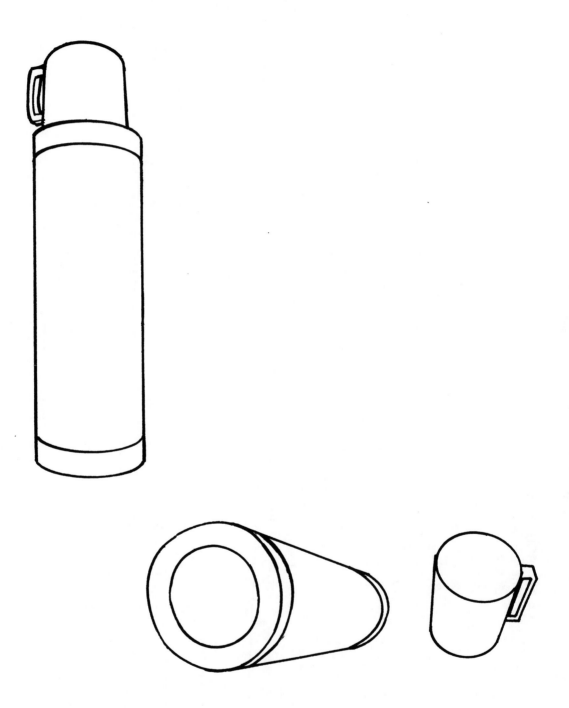

THINGS TO DO: Draw a small table and then draw a pail or a gallon of paint that has just fallen off the table.

ORTHOGRAPHIC PROJECTION OR PLAN PROJECTION
(ONE-POINT)

We will look at ONE-POINT PROJECTION as an introduction to a perspective method that approaches the technical/architectural drawings. ORTHOGRAPHIC PROJECTION isn't like the "freehand" drawings that we have been studying. It uses *exact* measurements and proportions. It is used mainly in industrial design, architecture, and so on. There will only be a couple of new terms to learn, so take heart.

PLAN: The view looking straight down on a form. There is absolutely no perspective to a PLAN.

STATION POINT: The distance of the observer from the object. This is very similar to the POINT OF STATION, which indicates the *height* of the observer's eye, or HL. Here we will show the *distance* as well and will call it the STATION POINT, or SP.

The problem:
We have a square PLAN and would like to see the three-dimensional view of it.

The solution:
1. Place the PLAN above the HORIZON LINE with one side of the PLAN touching the HL.

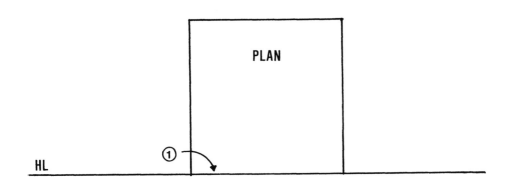

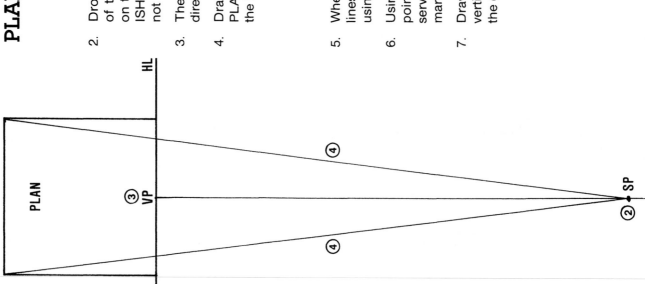

PLAN PROJECTION—ONE-POINT
(continued)

2. Drop a vertical center line from the front edge of the PLAN. Place the STATION POINT (SP) on this center line and below the HL. Like VAN-ISHING POINTS, the STATION POINT should not be to close to the HL.

3. The VANISHING POINT is located on the HL directly above the SP.

4. Draw lines from the SP to the corners of the PLAN; be sure to draw lines that do *not* touch the HL.

5. Where these lines cross the HL, draw vertical lines down toward the SP. Do the same thing using the corner points on the HL.

6. Using the vertical line that came from the corner point of the PLAN, mark a spot (X) that will serve as the base of the projection. Keep this mark a reasonable distance from the SP.

7. Draw a horizontal line that connects to the other vertical corner line. This represents the base of the cube.

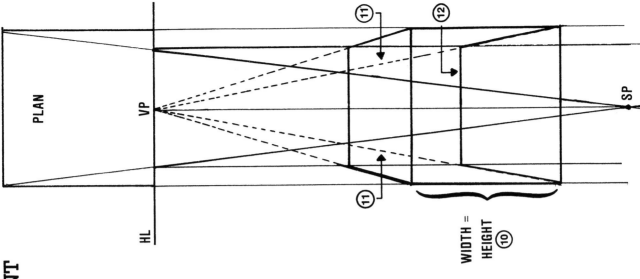

PLAN PROJECTION—ONE-POINT
(continued)

8. Draw PERSPECTIVE LINES from the VP to the corner points on the base line.

9. The points where these lines cross the other two vertical lines indicate the position of the other horizontal line, which will be the back base line. Draw the line.

10. The height of the CUBE will be the same measurement as the width, so that's easy enough to do. Draw the verticals and then the bottom horizontal line to complete the front face of the CUBE.

11. Your next step is to draw lines from the bottom corner points to the VP, where they intersect the vertical lines will be the spot for the last horizontal line.

12. Draw this horizontal line, which represents the back edge of the CUBE. You're done. In a dozen steps you have completed an ORTHOGRAPHIC PROJECTION. Congratulations! Now try a rectangle instead of a square.

PLAN PROJECTION—TWO-POINT

Here is one more term to be learned: ELEVATION. ELEVATION is defined as a straight-on view of one of the sides of the object. This view shows the height of the object. Note that none of the lines in an elevation view converge to a VANISHING POINT as they are always parallel to the observer.

HINT: As you learned in ONE-POINT ORTHO-GRAPHIC PROJECTION, you must estimate the STATION POINT. You should keep the SP well back from the PLAN you are projecting. A general rule of thumb is to keep the SP at least twice as far from the PLAN as the PLAN is wide.

1. Establish the HORIZON LINE (HL).

2. Place the corner of the PLAN on the HL. (Use a 30°-60°-90° triangle for this).

3. From the corner of the PLAN that touches the HL draw a vertical line. On this line establish the SP. (See HINT above.)

4. From the SP draw lines that are parallel to the sides of the PLAN until the lines meet the HL. Label one of these points VP(X) and the other VP(Y).

5. Draw PERSPECTIVE LINES (shown here as dash lines) from the SP to the different key points (corners, windows, door, etc.) that are on the PLAN. The illustration only shows the

left and right outside lines drawn to the SP while the others stop at the HL. The drawing will be less confusing this way.

6. Where the PERSPECTIVE LINES cross the HL, drop verticals.

7. Determine point A as the base of the front corner. (This is the same principle as the X in Lesson 50).

8. Draw a horizontal line through the point. This is the base of the structure.

9. The length and width of the PLAN are known dimensions as well as the height (ELEVA-TION). If the scale is 1/8 inch = 2 feet, then the PLAN shows a structure that is 44 feet long and 18 feet wide. The height of the structure is 15 feet. Therefore the ELEVATION will be 15/16 inch as shown in the illustration. The width of the ELEVATION will be the same width as the PLAN.

10. PERSPECTIVE LINES can now be drawn to finish the structure.

THINGS TO DO: Try a more complex set of plans using ORTHOGRAPHIC PROJECTION. (Suggestions: Try adding an ell or other addition to a PLAN.)

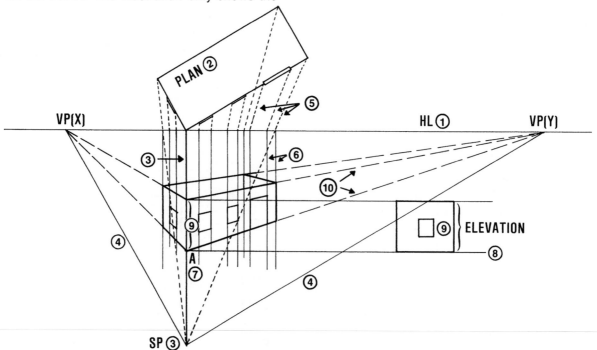

LETTERS IN PERSPECTIVE

I think you'll find that this is a project that combines almost everything about perspective and yet is very enjoyable. We're going to try the alphabet in perspective, and then you can add three-dimensional, solid shapes to the letters, and even some shadows, or reflections, or equal spacings, or any variety of perspective methods. Try using the initials in your name to come up with your own personalized logo. Try foreshortening some letters as well. I think you'll be surprised at the variety of techniques and finished art that not only *you*, but the whole class, can come up with. Show your art, look at other people's work, learn from your mistakes, but, above all, continue to practice. Before you know it, you probably won't need to do a lot of the preliminary perspective work that you do now. Practice will make you more observant.

APPENDIX
DEFINITIONS

AXIS (plural, AXES) An imaginary center line around which parts of a body or shape are symmetrically arranged, such as the earth's axis. Symmetrical objects have identical halves.

CUBE A cube is a regular solid of equal square sides. Dice are good examples of cubes.

DIAGONAL LINE A straight line from a corner to the opposite (diagonal) corner of a cube face, a rectangular face, a parallelogram, etc.

ELEVATION A straight-on view of one of the sides of a form in one-point perspective.

ELLIPSE The circle in perspective is called an ellipse. An ellipse has two axes, the major axis and the minor axis. (See "AXIS" above.) The major axis is always the longer of the two.

FORESHORTENING The change in shape of an object that leans or turns toward or away from the viewer.

GROUND LINE The base of the picture plane.

GROUND PLANE The ground plane is similar to the horizontal plane, except that it is at ground level and is the plane on which the object (as well as the viewer) is assumed to be resting.

HORIZON LINE/EYE LEVEL The horizon line is the same as the real horizon. The horizon line is also considered to be at the artist's eye level. If the horizon line cannot be seen because of obstructions it can be located by drawing a line at the artist's eye level.

HORIZONTAL LINE A straight line parallel to the horizon.

HORIZONTAL PLANE The observer, when viewing an object, sees it at eye level. That plane—from the observer's eyes through the horizon of the picture plane to the object—is the horizon plane.

INCLINED PLANE Any plane surface that is set at an angle against a horizontal surface; a sloping plane.

LINE OF VISION A straight line drawn from the station point to the point of sight.

ONE-POINT PERSPECTIVE (parallel perspective) One-point perspective occurs when rectangular forms are placed so that their sides are either parallel to the picture plane or perpendicular to it. There is one central vanishing point in one-point perspective.

PERPENDICULAR LINE A straight line drawn at a right angle to the horizontal line.

PERSPECTIVE (a different way of defining perspective) Perspective is a way of showing where the observer is. Objects don't have perspective—you, the observer, do.

PERSPECTIVE CENTER The center of an object's face is obtained by drawing two diagonal lines. Where they cross is the perspective center of that face or plane.

PERSPECTIVE LINES The lines from the edge and/or corner of an object that are extended to the horizon and its vanishing points.

PICTURE PLANE An imaginary transparent plane that is usually considered to be perpendicular to the ground. It is always perpendicular to the artist's line of sight, whether upward or downward. The drawing/painting surface normally represents the picture plane.

PLAN The view when looking straight down on a form. There is no perspective to a plan. It is similar to an architect's floor plans.

PLAN PROJECTION (or ORTHOGRAPHIC PROJECTION) The use of exact measurements, such as a floor plan and a front elevation, to construct a perspectively correct drawing.

POINT OF SIGHT The point on the horizon line opposite the station point (or eye of the observer).

STATION POINT (or POINT OF STATION) The point that represents the eye of the observer; on a perspective drawing, it shows the distance from the observer to the object.

THREE-POINT PERSPECTIVE (oblique perspective) A rectangular object positioned so that none of its edges are parallel to the picture plane is drawn in three-point perspective. Three vanishing points must be used. The left and the right vanishing points are used the same as in two-point perspective, but the verticals also merge to a third vanishing point.

TWO-POINT PERSPECTIVE (angular perspective) Two-point perspective is necessary when rectangular objects are positioned so that their faces are at an angle to the artist's line of sight. There are two vanishing points for an object in two-point perspective. If there are two cubes at different angles to the viewer, each cube will have its own vanishing points on the horizon. Vertical lines do not converge.

VANISHING POINT(S) The lines of an object, if extended perspectively toward the horizon, apparently meet at a point on the horizon line. A scene may have one or many vanishing points, but only one horizon line.

Lines that are on a plane parallel to the picture plane do not approach the horizon; therefore they do not converge and do not have a vanishing point.

VERTICAL LINE A straight line drawn at right angles to the horizon, running up and down.